FROM WHENCE I COMETH

POEMS

Charise A. Hepburn

DENVER, COLORADO

Outskirts Press, Inc.
http://www.outskirtspress.com

ISBN: 978-1-4787-5733-7

Library of Congress Registrion Number
TXu 1-923-274, 2014
VAu 1-084-316 – 12/2011 (Photographs)

Book Website
www.outskirtspress.com/fromwhenceicometh

Author's website
charisehepburn.com
Give feedback on the book at:
Charisehepburn@gmail.com

Outskirts Press and the "OP" logo are trademarks belonging to Outskirts Press, Inc.

PRINTED IN THE UNITED STATES OF AMERICA

for Janice

CONTENTS

PREFACE

We Tell Our Stories

a prayer...

we stand together, bonded by our pain
transitioning from what is past to what is future.
we remove the storm shutters from our heart
letting in the sunlight...

we choose to wear our scars in the open
to let others know they are not alone.
we bring to others hope and courage;
no longer invisible, we are the same...

we no longer hide in the shadows living in shame;
coming out from the darkness, vulnerable but stronger...
we tell our stories for those that feel
as if the world is closing in on them;
moving from one place in time to another...

we tell our stories to break the chains of bondage,
"yea, though I walk through the valley of the shadow of death"...
we are no longer afraid; we meet at this place
where there are no judgments,
no measurement of greater or lesser pain...

we tell our stories like a painter dipping rough bristles
into paint wells; spraying our souls across the sky,
like rainbows after a storm.
we are sisters, standing together,
heart to heart; telling our stories...

ONE

From Whence I Cometh

I know exactly the day the curse was cast,
It showed up cold and moist;
Red as the poinsettia,
Slowly trickling down between my thighs,
Staining my underwear.
What is this curse that I will carry way into my adult life?

Trapped in a cycle of twenty-eight days;
Twenty-eight days, starting with the beginning,
Twenty-eight days marking the next.
Plunged into a world taboo,
Unprepared for what was to come.
Haunted; Month after month...
Was I damned from the moment I was born?

I know why my mother prayed for boys,
Why she wished I was never born.
A curse, passed down through generations;
Her mother, her mother's mother...

What else was she to do but stand guard at the gate,
Questioning every missed period,
Protecting me from the inevitable,
From whence I cometh; A woman.
Driven by her mere existence,
In a world where her self-worth is questionable,
Valued by no one.

Was I to take on this world alone?
Thrown into battle without armor or shield;
Like Christians fighting in a coliseum
Surrounded by hungry lions, roaring,
Ready to devour flesh.

I hear the whispers of the willow tree,
Loud whispers of women before me,
They too want their stories told;
To have the curse removed.

Pain is my compass,
Loneliness is my friend,
Red is the color of the dirt that stains my feet
As I walk barefoot knowing that my mother,
Her mother and her mother's mother walk with me.
Blood red is the poinsettia.

The Day My Father Died

One by one...
They took us over to him,
In the order of our births and ranking;
First my mother,
Then each of my brothers,
Then my older sister...
Then me...

My father laid bare-naked on his deathbed,
A white sheet pulled halfway up his chest,
As if death had already arrived
And all that was left was to complete the ritual:
Closing of the eyes,
Covering of the face...

He grabbed my hand and stared at me
With yellow eyes; pupils so dark and small.
I could see his tongue moving; thick and heavy.
He was trying to say something to me,
But only mumbling sounds came out,
Buffered by the sounds of machines.

What was my father trying to tell me?
Was he trying to say that he loved me?
Though he had never said that to me
Or any of his children,
Nor had we expected it.

Maybe he was blaming me for his death.
After all, I was the one who prepared his meal
The day he fell out on the floor of our home.

I remembered, the meat smelled.
So angry with him, I cooked it anyway,
Cursing him under my breath.

Now haunted by my guilt,
I tried moving my hand away,
But death's grip was too strong.
I thought about the bread pudding I made earlier that day;
It had taken so long to bake that I had fallen asleep
Behind the sofa in the living room.

I recalled hearing a knock at the door; it had awakened me.
When I opened the door, no one was there...
They say, before a person dies the soul leaves the body
And travels to say goodbye to love ones.
My father had said goodbye to me,
With a knock on the door,
Hours before...

Still, I was not sure how to say goodbye to my father,
Now lying on his deathbed.
What was I supposed to say?
Was I to say that I love him?
Something I had never said to him,
Nor had he expected it.

I tried saying something; *I know I did.*
But all I heard were mumbling sounds; buffered...
Right then, someone hurried me out,
Then quickly rushed my little sister in.

Leaving Me

I collected the letters; all addressed to him.

His journals; where he detailed his daily life.

The note pads; where he scribbled his thoughts...

I remembered the letter from the woman who he had helped

She wrote; *please accept this sack of onions...*

There were many letters expressing gratitude; he was a kind man.

I remembered the rich white woman's letter; I had met her once.

She wrote; *the next time you want to come to the island,*

I will send our plane to get you.

Angry with my father for dying; leaving me without a father...

I collected them all; piled them in a heap outside

And set them on fire.

St. James Road

St. James Road was where my father's family lived in small
clapboard houses; Clustered together like oyster shells
washed out after a storm. Aunt Esther's house in front; green.
Aunt Titti behind her; yellow. Uncle Romeo; splitting image of
my father, his house to the right; orange, but sometimes green,
sometimes blue, depending on the leftover paint.
Aunt Charlotte in the back, blue; she and Aunt Titti fought all
the time. Seem like everywhere I stood were rocks hurting the
bottom of my feet. Dirt would creep out from between the rocks,
leaving my shoes gray and dusty. On hot days, when all fans were
circulating at full speed; bright color curtains would spring
to life and leap outside open windows, as if to add another splash of
paint to an already colorful heritage. I watched my father go
from house to house, dragging me along; white starched shirt,
dark creased pants and shiny white teeth morphing an unending smile.
Never forgetting from whence he had cometh.
Even as a little girl, I knew; this place called St James Road was
special and where my father was happiest… *amongst his family.*

September Slumber

In memory of Faith Elizabeth

I watched the leaf slowly fall to the ground.

Only a gentle wind carrying the leaf

To its resting place beneath the tree.

Autumn is upon us.

As I watched the leaf fall,

It seems to perform a final encore;

Bowing,

Twirling,

Spinning,

Sailing downwards...

Taking in the open space

One last time...

Yet again,

I find myself thinking of September

And wishing she was here.

But, I know now,

September sleeps beneath the tree,

Welcoming the fallen leaves.

Sleep my sweet September,

Sleep...

A New Beginning

I stood there facing her,
Only now aware of her nakedness;
Unmasked and stripped of all false pretense,
No more hidden secrets to reveal,
No more fear of being judged or ridiculed.
I could see the scars of battles won and lost,
Scars relentlessly burned into her flesh with a hot cast iron.
I whispered, I accept you;
I accept you broken and all.
No, I shouted... Woman!
As if to awake the woman in the mirror,
No more will I carry this burden;
A curse passed down through generations.
No more will I feel the guilt and shame of being a woman.
No more will I sit silently while others decide my fate.
No more,
No more,
I will claw my way out from this bottomless pit,
I will dig deep into its thick and charred lining
Until my fingers are bloodied and my knees scarred;
Swollen, red and burning,
I will rise,
I will rise,
I will look only towards the opening
Where the sun casts its light through the rocks;
There I will find a cool drink of water.
I will look to a new beginning...

TWO

The Beating of Abigail

Everyone who was up early that Saturday morning heard the screams;
Screams of someone being beaten half to death.
Dragged by her father from her bed to the outdoor toilet,
All because Abigail had gotten pregnant.
Everyone who was up early that Saturday morning heard the screams;
Beaten...
People closed their windows to shut out the sounds,
Hid behind closed doors to avoid getting involved,
Some even thought;
That would teach Abigail not to fool around with boys.

Lord, have mercy, Abigail screamed out,
Hoping someone would come and save her,
But no one came to rescue Abigail,
Everyone pretended it was not happening.
Her father hit her again with such force, almost killing her,
Then he stepped outside onto the propped-up toilet step,
He, exhausted from the beating.
He stopped, as if to breathe in the morning air;
Stained with blood,
Then he spit and leisurely walked back to his house,
As if he had only just taken a leak.

No one saw Abigail leave the outdoor toilet that day,
No one saw her make her way back to the house,
No one saw her stumble to the ground weak from the beating,
No one...

No one saw her torn and bloody clothes,

Nor did they see the shame on her swollen face,

Or the bruises that would forever stay with her.

But everyone heard the screams that Saturday morning;

Beaten...

All because Abigail had gotten pregnant.

Wandering Hands

I knew something was wrong.

I could feel his gloved finger,

Wandering,

Penetrating me.

Frozen,

Paralyzed,

Too afraid to move.

Why didn't I do something.

Jumped off the examination table,

Pushed him away,

Scream...

Long after the examination; the violation,

Long after the prescription was filled,

I could still feel his body pressed against me,

Leaning in from the side of the table;

Touching me...

I could still hear the sound of his low and slow breathing,

Smell the strong scent of his cologne,

A stench soon replaced with my shame;

A shame, I will carry forever.

I wonder how many young girls are molested by their doctor...

The Altar Boogeyman

sea grapes

    coco plums

blue ocean

    hopscotch

nursery rhymes...

    winding path that led to the house on the hill

    where the priest lived...

    I do not know your name

    you were always there taking care of the yard

    you did not look like the boogeyman in the stories

    boogeymen don't serve on altars

        or do they?

"a candy bar if you pull down your panties"

    that was what you said to me

    the day I followed you inside...

The Road to the Abortion

The sudden honk of the car horn outside
Reminded me of a starter's pistol,
Causing my heart to leap outside my chest;
I swear, I saw my own heart expanding, contracting,
Right in front of me.
The alert has sounded; time to run towards the finish line.
But where is that finish line?
Is it when I walk through the clinic's door?
Or when I leave with my womb barren?

I know my guilt will hold me prisoner,
Damned to hell without reprieve...

I did not notice the overcast day.
I did not see the woman on the corner with her child,
Neither did I notice the jogger out early that morning
Momentarily running alongside the car.
I wanted only to look ahead,
Stay on the path;
A path that I know I will have much regret.

No words were spoken on the ride there; just complete silence.
Except for the occasional blinking sound;
Right turn, wrong turn...
I silently prayed.
Prays to Mother Mary and her son, Jesus Christ,
Begging for forgiveness for taking this road;
A road that is long and difficult.

Hate That Poisons

What makes a person hate so much?
Walking around with all this poison inside.
Pain building up inside,
Manifesting and turning into rage.
Bottled, sealed tight,
Ready to implode.

You have cried out in pain but no one heard your cries.
You tried masking it with gold and silver,
But its corpse remained;
Decaying,
Festering with maggots in a rotten carcass,
Leaving behind a fowl and poisonous stench.

Old age will be here in the morning,
Soon death will be upon us,
Galloping-in with speed on a white horse,
Across land and through valleys,
Where the river banks glisten at sunset.
Now is the time,
Now is the time,
Before it's too late.

Oxygen

What is it about sibling rivalry that causes me to gasp for air?

Only a matter of time before another fight,

Before another door is slammed,

Another call is disconnected

Leaving a static disturbance without signal.

I screamed inside until my lungs are empty.

Until I cannot breathe.

Is it fear?

Fear of losing,

Self...

Tribe...

Holding on to an unforgiving past;

Refusing to conform.

Harsh words spoken,

Misunderstanding rampant,

No one stopping,

No one listening,

Daggers with jagged edges

Penetrating the heart,

Shouts...

Screams...

Oxygen!

I cannot breathe.

Broken Family

Lately, I have been racking my brain,
Trying to remember,
When we stopped being a family...
I remember the Sunday dinners,
The joy of getting together,
The older ones showing of their skills;
The correct way to use a fork and knife,
At times with an impressive flick of the wrist.
I remember fighting over who gets the leg or the gizzard,
Losing every time to sibling's ranking,
Always remembering to save space for mom's pound cake
Or sister's lemon meringue pie.
I remember the fun monopoly games,
The competitive card games of spades,
Classical music on the turntable,
Someone eventually passed out on the couch,
Preserved by thick plastic; snoring.
I remember my brothers arguing over baseball;
Roberto Clemente is the greatest player ever lived...
Fans oscillating towards my brothers' heated arguments,
Two, three of them at times; all circulating hot air.
Laughter,
More Laughter,
Good times...
But, for the life of me,
I cannot remember,
When we stopped being a family.

Denial

My mother hit me with an empty soda bottle,

then with the broomstick,

she told me I will never amount to anything

and wished that I was dead.

I asked her many years later,

when I became a woman,

why she did those things

and said such awful words,

she denied it all,

and that was that...

The Photograph

I opened the drawer and pulled out the old photograph,
    It is the only image that I have of the family together.

I gently touched it,
    Trying not to cause any more tears.

The oldest at the center,
    Elevated...

Others with their plates extended towards him.
    Such irony...

Reaching for a serving of a legacy,
    Left behind.

Trusting,
    For what should be bestowed to them.

After All These Years

I would like to think that after all these years,
    The bitterness that consumed you,
    Eating away at your core,
    No longer existed.
        But that would not be the case.

I would like to think I know of a place,
    Somewhere in the Sahara desert,
    Where water flows upstream,
    Where there are never sand storms
    Hindering us from moving forward,
        But that too, would not be the case.

So I accept these hard and difficult truths,
    I choose to breathe in the air around me,
    To take care of me first,
    To not expect but to accept,
        So I may love me and love you.

Rosanna

Rosanna comes to me dressed in black; dark and mysterious.
When she is with me I am drunk in her spell,
Intoxicated by her dance;
A slow dance that gets deep into my head.

Some people call her depression; I call her Rosanna.
She is like a jazz singer scatting,
Beckoning me; *come dance with me.*
Filling my loneliness with a peaceful comfort.

Even when I toss and turn all night, disturbed by her presence,
She gets me up in the morning and lets me go about my day,
Like a functioning addict;
An addict without drugs to ease the pain.

When I was a child I wanted to be crazy.
I know a few crazy people, they never needed excuses,
People just called them crazy.
But I am sane...

So I learn to hide my pain,
Bending and swaying amongst the bamboo trees
Floating weightlessly; like in space.

Then without warning she blows me a kiss goodbye,
But I know she will be back
And I will dance again with Rosanna.

THREE

On the Road to Alabama

Lord, why am I on this road again,
What do I need to learn; is it humility?
Here I am, my car piled to the hills,
My dog whimpering in the backseat,
He realizes we are miles away from his favorite park.
Somewhere on I-85 is a truck with all my stuff;
Clothes long outdated, desperate to hold on to what is familiar,
I packed everything...
Why Lord, am I on this road again?
To a place I know I will not come to love.

I turned the dial on the radio just in time to hear the preacher shout,
Jesus saves!
Save me God from this hell,
Where racism and bigotry lurk on every corner;
Disguised but present.
Reminding me of the time in Birmingham;
Dogs, water hoses, children, people dying...
Jesus saves!
The preacher hammering the point.
Occasionally an interruption of country music
Seeps through the airwaves like an unexpected breeze.
What was I thinking accepting this job?
Letting my desperation overwhelm me,
Taking me to this God-forsaken place call Alabama,
Where angry dogs lie and wait; ready to devour flesh.
Still I forged ahead, like a lost child being led by the hand,
Deeper into the South...

What is it about cornfields that remind me of my own loneliness?

Each corn stalk rustling in the wind yet remaining firm,

Bounded together like family.

Yet, when I look out upon its vastness,

From which I stand,

Alone,

Fighting,

Resisting,

I cannot help but to think of my own isolation,

My unwillingness to conform to others belief of who I should be;

Not accepting who I am...

How many of "you" do I need to be before I am accepted?

I crossed into Georgia just as the August sun began to bake me alive,

Soon I will be at hell's gate.

I could hear already the snarling of the dogs,

The rattling of the chains,

Hoses being pulled from iron rods,

The screams of ghosts from their graves;

Mothers,

Fathers,

Children...

Please God be merciful,

I will be faithful,

I will be humble...

A Woman I Met in Alabama

I met a woman at a gas station in Alabama,

She was white

and middle-aged.

She wore a plain A-line dress

and spoke with a deep Southern accent.

She asked me a question,

something about working the gas pump...

I looked at her for a moment

and saw a woman just like me,

Someone needing a helping hand.

That surprised me.

She Is Life

Life is like the soul of a woman.
She is gentle and nurturing.
She is like a flower that blooms in springtime
and like the morning rays that greets us
Reminding us that a new day is here.
She is the calm that delivers us through stormy times.

She is our mothers,
Our sisters,
Our grandmothers,
Our wives,
Our daughters,
She is the soul of a woman...

She is Harriet,
Anne, Ella,
Sojourner, Rosa
Emily, Josephine
and Maya...
She is larger than life...

She is the woman who goes unnoticed.
Who arrives at the close of the business day,
To empty our garbage bins
and sweeps away the crumbs
Fallen beneath our desks.
Crumbs from our broken lives...

She is the single mother working two jobs to feed her children,
She is the young mother waiting in line at the grocery store,
With the screaming child pulling at her skirt tail,
While we hastily cast judgment and show impatience.
She is definitely life...

When we think we have learned everything about life,
She offers us another lesson,
At times knocking us off our feet,
Reminding us of what may have been forgotten...
To be kind,
To be patience,
To be good,
To be grateful, to love, to forgive...
She is what humbles us...
She is Life!

On the Road from Alabama

As I merged onto Interstate 21, I could see in my rearview mirror
the Alabama lilac morning sky,
Reminding me of the wisteria that blossom in the spring;
Hanging along the roadside like grapes on vines,
I whispered,
God, what was it you wanted me to learn?
Was it humility?

My car now packed to the hills,
My dog whimpering in the backseat;
He realizes we are miles from his favorite park.
I too will miss the park where we would go and watch
The orange sunset turn to red; blood red,
Then disappear into the horizon.

I will remember the Sunday brunches,
Sitting outside eating brioche and sipping on mimosas...
Imaging that I was somewhere along the French Rivera,
Anywhere, except Alabama...
I whispered a prayer to God.
Was it gratitude?

Miles and miles away from Alabama,
I thought about my neighbors behind;
The woman who had a double mastectomy,
The man whose wife left him stranded along a Louisiana highway,
Only to return to an empty place,

The young woman downstairs and her many suitors;
The flowers left at her door.
God, how I envied her youth...

The August sun tapped against my windshield
As I crossed over into Georgia,
Just as the speed limit slowed to a halt.
I slowed my car down and slipped Ray into the CD drive;
Georgia on my mind...
Cops in this part of the South frighten me.

I thought about the racism I encountered;
White people, Black people discriminating...
I thought about the many people I would see
Spitting from moving vehicles along Route 280;
Big flying wads of spit...
I glanced over in time to see a yellow antique car pull off the highway;
Always a white middle-aged dude driving one of these things...

Day soon worn into night,
The car headlights streamed along the road in front of me,
Alabama, now hundreds of miles behind me.
Still I find myself thinking of her lilac morning sky,
Her mountainous views and blood-red sunsets,
Her bigotry and hopelessness,
All lingering on...
Goddamn Alabama!

If I Should Die

Ode to the Bahamas

If I should die,
O let it be in the arms of my country,
Let me walk barefoot along her sandy shores
And watch the seagulls skirt her waves,
Wings spread wide,
Soaring high into the clouds,
Then back again,
Diving into the sea...

If I should die,
O let it be in the arms of my country,
Let me hear the laughter of the children,
Echoing like musical sounds from afar
And recall the times when I was once a child,
So happy,
So free...

If I should die,
O let it be in the arms of my country,
Let me gaze into her blue skies,
With arms outstretched,
Soaking in the sunrays upon my face
Welcoming her warm embrace.
Soon...
She will carry me home.

If I should die,
O let it be in the arms of my country,

Let me be still for a moment,
And listen to the rhythms of the tide
Constant beating against the rocks;
Rhythms of life;
Life's sugary kisses,
Bittersweet...

If I should die,
O let it be in the arms of my country,
Let me stare into her horizon
Way, way over yonder,
Where the ocean meets the sky;
Blue beneath the red velvet kiss,
Purple-rising...
Let me watch the sun set upon her majestic beauty
And know that heaven awaits me...

 If I should die,
O let it be in the arms of my country,
Let me lay upon her bosom like a child,
While she gently rocks me to sleep.
Let my heart beat in time with the goatskin drums,
Fading,
Rising,
Fading...
   into the night.

The Hag

Late one night, I saw a hag,

She was dressed in all white,

Her skin was old and weathered,

Her body emaciated by life's experiences.

As she crossed the street in front of my car,

I could see a ghostly veil of dust covering her face.

With eyes sunken, cold and lifeless,

She stared me dead in the eye,

Sending a shiver that seeped deep into my bones...

Was she warning me or cursing me?

I will never know.

As I drove away, I checked my rearview mirror and she was gone,

Only darkness remained;

Darkness of what was yet to come.

FOUR

Nameless

I.

Why can't I remember her name?
I remember the whispers of incest...
At first, I did not understand.
Confused, I asked:
How could that happen?
They are church people;
Her father is a deacon.

II.

Each time we walked by the house,
I would hear her crying;
Low moans that pierced my childhood heart.
Once I thought I saw her looking out
Through a crack in the boarded-up window.
One day, I asked my mother about her,
She told me that her parents had locked her away
Because she was sick in the head.
I didn't understand what that meant, but I felt sad.

III.

A girl came out of a white van one day,
Her hair was unkempt,
Her once white dress looked dingy,
An older man dragged her alone.
For a few seconds she looked directly at me;
Did I see a look of despair?
Was she asking for my help?

43

I drove around the parking lot several times,
Disturbed by her stare,
Conflicted;
Should I call the police?
What if I am wrong?
Eventually, I drove away,
Doing nothing....
I am still haunted by her stare.

IV.
As I walked down Madison Avenue,
I overheard a conversation behind me,
Two business men bragging,
About having sex with a 14 year old girl;
Pedophiles in suits.

V.
I traveled all the way to the Caribbean
To see a fat old tourist with a young local girl.
She wore a mini skirt and high kneel shoes,
A weave that was freshly done,
I am sure, paid for by the fat old tourist;
A bone to entice her into his sick and pathetic mind.
You know when a girl is being used inappropriately.
I wanted to scream out loud:
What are you doing?

Without Self

Naked,
He dragged me to the mirror,
We had just finished making love,
I thought.
See, how fat you are,
He shouted.

Ashamed,
I pulled away,
Not wanting to look at my Self in the mirror,
Never wanting to look at her again.
Afraid;
Afraid that I may hate her...

Desperate,
My own desperation.
I returned to his bed,
Without Self,
Seeking his love,
Wanting to be loved.

After the Numbness

There is a moment of insanity that happens
right after the numbness wears off.
It is the moment when you feel you can
no longer survive in this world as it is;
Along, without him...

When the air is so thick you cannot breathe.
When the pain begins to gnaw away at you,
leaving a cavity of decay;
Deep and rotten...

Have you ever had a headache that never
reaches its full potential?
Just hangs around driving you insane;
A limbo of insanity...

I lie still in the darkness,
pretending to be dead;
Sleep is welcome now...

Lost Souls

I know it was summer because the days were long.

I had come to him, lost and tormented, desperate for

his comfort. It was the only place I could go

and not be judged. He took the vinyl record out of

its case and put Roy Hamilton on the turntable;

"You'll never walk alone", streamed through the speakers.

My vulnerability exposed, laid naked before him.

Rays of sunlight slipped through the thick curtains

and purposely fell upon us. We embraced the comfort

of the light like children feeding on their mother's breast.

I remembered when I brought a lover home to his bed;

The same week I wrecked his sports car; red...

Sitting at the kitchen table eating sweet-and-sour chicken;

This seemed appropriate for the bitter-sweetness of our love.

He told me of how he saw me with my lover and forgave me.

His drunkenness often misunderstood. But I knew

it was the only way he could deal with his pain,

Then he would tell me of how he met his soulmate,

but lost her to another man a long time ago...

Intoxicated by his stories, we both were lost,

Only to be rescued by the comfort of each other's love.

Ten Women Speak of Abuse

1.

It may surprise you but I do not love my husband,
I stopped loving him years ago,
It is the children that keep us together.

2.

I am trapped in his web of manipulation;
Nothing that I feel, think or do is mine.
My mere existence belongs to him.
Why do I let him destroy me?

3.

Seven years and then some,
Seven more years to recover,
Finally, I am liberated...

4.

You look at me, my sister
With all my wounds and scars,
You ask me why I let him beat me.
I say to you, my sister,
Have you ever known this type of love?

5.

I screamed, he is going to kill me,
He grabbed me by my hair and shouted;
"Shut up bitch".

6.

I fell down the stairs,
That is what I will tell them,
I fell down the stairs...

7.

I told my mother, my father raped me.
She called me a lying slut.

8.

I am silence
Because I am afraid of him

9.

I wish I had a gun,
I would kill him.

10.

Who cares about my pain?
"No one cares about you",
That is what he keeps telling me.

FIVE

Zahir Morning Dawns

For Vivette

Zahir comes to me in the mornings
In my dreams,
And when I wake.
As I go about my business

Readying myself,
There you are waiting in the mist,
Where angels go to weep.
When you left that morning,

I became so enraged with anger,
I did not have time to grieve,
Overwhelmed with pain,
Suffocated by my guilt of knowing

I wanted to terminate the pregnancy.
But the moment you arrived,
I loved you unconditionally,
You showed me your beautiful soul

For only a little while. Then you
Drifted away as quietly as
You had come. A kiss goodbye,
Upon the early morning lilac sky.

Ripping my heart out,
Condemning me to hell, cursed.

Undeserving of love; the cobblestone
Beneath my feet burned hot. Then one day,

You broke through my darkness
Like early morning dawn,
Breathing a gentle dew
Upon my window sill.

You whispered,
I am here with you,
I have never left,
I will see you in the morning dawns.

Strange Dream

As I was walking down the street
I met a man name Paul.
He was white, handsome,
Dark hair and had a beautiful smile.
We talked for a while and he told me,
He owned a place called Le Bouchon,
Or maybe it was another French name.
He told me that he had a cake mixer to sell to me;
Two hundred and sixteen dollars...
I told him I will buy it on Friday.
Then we said goodbye.

The next day I went to Le Bouchon
And asked for the proprietor.
A man came out that looked like Paul
But this time he was black.
He came around to where I stood,
Told me of the wonderful things his mixer can do;
Turn this knob for bread and this knob for cake,
Pull here, push there; on and on,
With much delight.

Suddenly, we were traveling along a dark road,
Holding hands and talking about our problems.
But now, he was neither black nor white.
He told me of his brother's drug use
I told him of my distaste for Corporate America.

The road turned into a narrow sandy path
With a hilly and wooded terrain on one side,
Strangely, the ocean on the other side...
I could see flood lights streaming from a car ahead...
Then he told me that he had to leave;
It was not safe for him,
I did not understand right then...

Without warning he turned into a white deer
With small brown spots then leapt into the woods.
I tried following but the hilly terrain was too steep to climb...
I ran along the bottom path calling out his name;
Paul, Paul...
Hoping that he was running somewhere beside me,
Hidden by the woods.
Just when I thought I heard him calling my name
I woke up...

Seven Buckets of Water

I watched you carry the buckets of water,
All seven, filled to the rim.
You carried the first one upon your head,
Never swaying or bending, only staying strong.
Then you returned
And carried two more buckets of water,
This time you placed them on your shoulders.
I imagined your load must have been heavy,
But never once did I hear you complain.

You walked along the hot tarred road,
Then across the sunbaked fields.
I saw you set down the buckets to rest for a while,
But then quickly you started up again;
You knew there was no time to waste
And that your journey would be long.
You needed to carry all seven buckets
Before the setting of the sun.

Two more, then another and yet another...
It was as if they were not buckets of water
But pillows filled with feathers.
Masking your pain,
Hiding your struggles;
I know of the many sacrifices made,
Never once regretting.

Somebody asked,
Where are you going so weighted down?
You smiled and replied;
Across the fields and over the hills,
Where the sun kisses the heavens,
And the rivers flow with milk and honey.
Where the meadows green and lively,
Where the flowers bloom all year round
And the honeysuckle perfumes the air.
There, you will find me, in Paradise,
Watching over my seven buckets of water;
All filled to the rim.

September No More

"The Passing"

Broken heart in pieces,
Memories that never fade,
Night arrived like a galloping horseman.
The candle glow has faded,
September is no more.

Joy suspended; sorrow ushered in,
Tears that fall like rain.
Puddles reflecting beneath
The withered rose garden.
September is no more...

Lord, have mercy,
Heal my broken heart,
Be present another tomorrow;
I pray...
September is no more.

Reflection

A woman stopped me on the street the other day,

Asking for some change.

As I handed her the coins from the bottom of my bag,

I saw in her eyes a reflection of me.

I Remember

I remember it like yesterday, the dresser where she stood,
the picture frame to the right, the small ceramic dish
with her pearl earrings. I close my eyes and there she is
again; all dressed for church. I see her smelling the different

perfumes; deciding on which one goes with which hat.
Calling one of the children to catch the pearls in the back,
Then a gentle touch at the neckline; *they are still there*. I can
clearly see the pink and green floral curtains tucked at one end.

I see her sitting at the edge of the bed looking out of the window,
every so often talking to the children outside or shooing the
dogs away. The hat boxes neatly stacked along the closet shelf,
The shoes lined-off against the closet wall. The mint green suit,

the blue skirt, the many church dresses; everything
cleaned and pressed.   I will never forget how her handbag
hung on the closet door. Nor will I forget how she insisted
on buying a bag with many pockets inside to hold her things;

candies to suck-on during church service, a white pressed handkerchief
neatly folded inside, coins to handout to the kids; to buy something
sweet at the corner store. A few dollars hidden away inside
for the man who took the garbage cans to the road. I see the radio

on the nightstand, her bible to read the scriptures, the telephone,
one time such an integral part of her life; calling her sisters,

checking on her children; towards the end, just a fixture
on a nightstand, no one else to call. The windows that once would

let in the cool breeze are closed now, the doors are blotted,
the grass has grown tall, the pears have fallen to the ground
and left to rot, the garden needs weeding, the gate swings open...
Mama is gone and nobody lives there anymore.

Benediction

We kneel
We pray
We wait
For the bells
To toll
For the light
To descend
For hearts exposed
Upon an altar
We kneel
We pray
We wait
For the bells
To toll
For the light
To ascend
To show
Us the way

Photos From:

Potters Cay Wharf
Collection

Acknowledgements

I would like to express my gratitude to the many friends that encouraged me on this poetic journey; to all those that provided support and an ear to listen to unsolicited readings during the writing process.

I want to thank my son, Roimon, my biggest supporter; you were one of the first to tell me to write the book because you understood the importance of healing better than I did.

Thanks to Janice, my confidant and friend, to whom I dedicated this book and to whom I am never afraid to be completely honest.

Finally, thanks to all those reading my poems and can relate... I am humbled.

"Like a painter dipping rough bristles into paint wells;
spraying our souls across the sky...
standing together heart to heart; telling our stories"

About The Author

Charise Hepburn was born in The Bahamas and relocated with her son to the United States in 1985. In 2011, Charise published a book of her photography entitled; My Junkanoo, which captured images of a cultural celebration in the Bahamas.

This collection of poems is her first poetry book and deals with a woman's struggle, loss and the feeling of despair including those from her own experiences.

Charise currently works in Information Technology and lives in Charlotte, North Carolina with her dog Yiska.

Image Created by Charise Hepburn ©

CPSIA information can be obtained at www.ICGtesting.com
Printed in the USA
BVOW08s0212240915

419493BV00001B/51/P